Protestantism

by
Dr Cyprian Blamires

*All booklets are published thanks to the
generous support of the members of the
Catholic Truth Society*

CATHOLIC TRUTH SOCIETY
PUBLISHERS TO THE HOLY SEE

2

Contents

Who are the Protestants?

The origins: Western Christians reject papal supremacy

It is easier to say who Protestants are than what Protestantism is. The term 'Protestant' was applied historically to persons belonging to one of several rival European movements of thought and practice with one thing at least in common: they all preached or assumed that it was possible - and indeed desirable - for true followers of Christ to abandon their traditional allegiance to the Bishops of Rome as successors to St Peter. Over the ten centuries of the Church's history prior to the sixteenth century Protestant Reformation there had been only one major global division in Christendom – that between West and East. This corresponded roughly speaking to the modern fault line between Catholicism in western Europe and the Orthodox Churches in the east. During the Middle Ages there were numerous tensions within the western church and some of these involved movements that were condemned by the authorities of the Church as heretical (eg. the Albigensians, also known as Cathars). But it was not until the sixteenth century that very significant territorial areas, communities and individuals in western Europe were taken by their secular rulers, partly under the influence of Protestant preachers, completely outside the obedience of the bishops of Rome. This was one major effect of the movement of religious thought and practice now known as the Protestant Reformation.

Since then of course Protestantism has spread far beyond the confines of Europe and all over the globe. However, in practice a Protestant today may still be defined very broadly either as a European Christian outside both the Roman and the Orthodox obedience, or as a member of one of the denominations or movements in other parts of the world whose roots are to be found (however remotely) in the Reformation movement in western Europe. Not all of those who fit this description are happy to be labelled 'Protestant' however, as we shall see later on.

The spectrum of Protestantism

The spectrum of belief and practice of Protestants in the world today is truly vast. It encompasses equally the formal liturgies of the Lutheran and Anglican state churches – which retain many similarities with Catholic liturgy – along with their Catholic-style Episcopal hierarchies; and the tiny house-church congregation meeting in someone's front room. Here there is no ordained pastorate or formal hierarchy but just a group meeting to praise God in singing and prayer, to make intercession for others, to break bread on occasion in memory of the Last Supper, and to grow in understanding of the bible through sermons and exposition. Whereas two hundred years ago the state church version of Protestantism was very much in the ascendancy, this ascendancy has increasingly come into question in modern times. The advent of a global mass media makes a national religion look somewhat limited, and the ascendancy since the sixties of a culture of informality and cosiness makes a set liturgy look archaic. Even in the Church of England, where for centuries the Prayer Book services were the only liturgical forms in use, adherence to the 'official' set liturgies has become increasingly tenuous, with the growth of a tendency to a 'do it yourself' worship service. Some clergy do not wear robes or vestments at all for services and there is a certain preference for the 'hymn sandwich' type of worship (prayers and a sermon with hymns in between). Television influence is also noticeable with a tendency to hold local 'Songs of Praise' services modelled on the television 'Songs of Praise' programme. In the meantime the sixties cultural tendencies mentioned above have encouraged many to leave formal 'mainstream' religion and join movements less 'hampered' by formal liturgies or traditions.

Protestants and unity

There is no single body in the world that represents
Protestantism or Protestants in the way that the Pope and
the bishops can be said to represent Catholicism and
Catholics. Many Catholics cannot understand this and
find themselves bewildered by the sight of so many
different movements, creeds, and doctrines within
Protestantism. There is one Catholic Church but there are
many Protestant churches. Most Protestants on the other
hand do not nowadays regard the existence of a single
organisation of Christians as a good thing, indeed for
many of them it is positively harmful. What Catholics
prize as the precious unity of the Church, Protestants look
on as a colourless and mechanical uniformity imposed
from above. This represents something of a departure
from earlier attitudes; as recently as 1961 an apologist for
Protestantism could write: 'We cannot disguise the fact
that there are skeletons as well as treasures in the
Protestant closet. The skeleton most difficult to hide is
contemporary Protestantism's divided character ...'
(Robert McAfee Brown, *The Spirit of Protestantism*, New
York: Galaxy, 1965 [1961], p. 24)

Protestants have been at the heart of the ecumenical
movement and this in itself seems to suggest that they
must be looking for a unified world church. But to
assume that would be to misunderstand the goal of

Protestant ecumenism. For Catholics there cannot be any unity apart from the See of Rome and unity must involve some sort of realignment with the See of Rome. But for Protestants the goal of ecumenism is something much looser, it is an idea of a federation of churches in which each church would preserve its own special charisms while being enabled to engage in coordinated action with other Christians in certain areas. The idea that this must in some way involve a realignment with Rome might be acceptable to some, but for many it would be at best an irrelevance, at worse a dangerous snare.

The Recovery of the 'Pure' Original Gospel at the Reformation

The difference of outlook here between Catholic and
Protestant is absolutely fundamental, and it makes an
excellent starting-point in the quest to understand what
Protestantism considers it stands for. The Protestant of
today glories in the multiplicity of denominations and
movements not because he does not believe in Christian
unity, but because he has a different idea of what
Christian unity is. For Protestants, unity is essentially
something inward, something in the heart, *rather than*
something outward and external. Protestants believe in
an invisible unity known only to God, a unity that is
more real and more powerful than any external unity
within a single institution would be. This preference for
an inner *invisible* unity takes us to the heart of what
Protestantism is about. Protestants believe that they have
a mission to uphold truly 'spiritual' values not simply
over against a 'materialistic' world that pays no attention
to God, but also over against a 'materialistic' Catholic
Church which has lost sight of these values. Their
argument runs like this. The gospel was revealed
by Christ and in Christ and was lived out directly,

simply, and obediently by the first Christians as
described in the Acts of the Apostles. Unfortunately that
early enthusiasm and freshness and simplicity of the
divinely-revealed gospel progressively disappeared from
view as man-made rules, ordinances, and practices
became more important in the Church. Generally
speaking Protestants allow that the first three or four
hundred years of the Church's existence were years
when the gospel was still understood and known about,
and the supreme achievement of this first period was the
creation of the Creeds. These are considered to represent
simple and unvarnished summaries of what the Christian
faith is about, and they are also widely believed to be
sufficient statements of Christian belief. If something is
not in the bible or in those early creeds, then, the
argument runs, it cannot be imposed on the conscience
of any Christian.

The way Protestants see things, the gospel was taught
in all its fullness to the early Christians. Following this,
they spent those first centuries both sorting out which
texts were to be considered as divine revelation to be
included in the holy book, and drawing lines around true
apostolic belief (orthodoxy) so as to exclude what was
not believed to be compatible with that (heresy or
heterodoxy). But after the main lines of the faith had been
set out in those early centuries, a disturbing and
destructive development set in. In their understanding of

what happened to the Church after the early centuries of revelation and consolidation Protestants diverge very radically from Catholics.

The 'corruption' of the gospel by the medieval Church

Protestantism is built on the belief that something went badly wrong in the Church after the first four or five centuries. Their account of Church history runs like this. That original spiritual divine message which turned the world upside down became gradually overlaid by something else, something man-made. Although attempts were made here and there to recover the original divine deposit - and predecessors had been feeling their way towards the goal over the previous two centuries (eg the Englishman John Wycliffe (1324-1384) and the Czech John Hus (1369-1415)) - it was only at the Protestant Reformation that the work was completed. The Protestant Reformers finally recovered the jewel of that pristine original gospel revelation from out of the dross which had come to veil its beauty and splendour. The early Reformers did not necessarily wish to separate from the Catholic Church on account of this, but they found themselves obliged to do so because the Pope and the hierarchy could not accept their understanding of what this primitive gospel was. 'Luther and his followers put fidelity to the gospel above fidelity to medieval ecclesiasticism' (McAfee Brown, *op. cit.*, p. 25).

According to the followers of the Reformers, the early Christians taught a simple gospel of repentance before God and acceptance of divine forgiveness won for us through the sacrifice of Christ on our behalf. They met together, as the New Testament tells us, to sing psalms and spiritual songs, and they repeated the last supper of Christ together as he commanded when he said 'Do this in remembrance of me'. Unfortunately, instead of holding fast to such basic divinely-revealed teachings and practices, the Catholic Church elaborated the 'man-made' sacramental system. To Protestants, this system seems to be about having to undergo a series of rituals in order to obtain salvation and eternal life. The way Protestants see the Catholic approach, as long as they are duly baptised and confirmed, attend mass and confession regularly and have a Christian burial, believers are encouraged to trust that they will be saved. This is seen by Protestants as the acme of 'mechanical' religion in which the response of the heart to the love of Christ has no place.

Though the Catholic hierarchy had no problem with the idea that the study of the early church could provide huge inspiration for every generation, they did not think in terms of 'going back' to the early church as the Reformers did. For Catholics the faith was indeed divinely revealed in Christ to the Apostles, but the Church does not make a strict division between the 'purity' of the early church and the 'corruption' of later generations. Rather, the Church sees the divine deposit given to the Apostles and their successors in the early days as a treasure chest available for exploration and enjoyment by later generations. Each of those later generations drew more jewels out of that original deposit. Someone who inherits a magnificent estate replete with many acres of land and properties cannot assimilate it all at one glance; he needs time to discover what is there and to ascertain what are the items of most value. The land will also produce further crops, generation by generation. For the Catholic that original revelation was like a fertile soil in which many beautiful plants, shrubs, and trees have grown up over time. The seeds were there from the beginning, but it took time for them to germinate. As to the sacramental system, the Church has never doubted that it could be misunderstood in the way described; but equally she has never believed that mechanical performance of rituals is enough for salvation. For all the Catholic saints, the sacraments have been the starting-point for growth in faith and love for Jesus, not the full package.

What then is the recovered divine 'original' message which Protestants see themselves as called to preach and defend in the world today? Underneath all the vast differences between the multifarious Protestant movements certain common features of this message can be uncovered.

'Spiritual' versus 'mechanical' religion

All Protestant movements assume that they are promoting a truly 'spiritual' religion. This is very puzzling to Catholics, who normally assume that they are doing the same. But it is the explanation for many things which surprise Catholics in Protestantism. Most Protestant churches and chapels are more or less bare of ornaments, pictures, and religious artefacts like crucifixes and statues. (Where such items exist, it is generally because the building is a historic one which has been inherited by Protestants from the medieval Catholic Church.) This seems to Catholics to be something negative, but for Protestants it is making a positive statement. The message is that the believer is to focus his thoughts not on the outward attractions of pictures, statues, and beautiful buildings, but on what is going on in his heart. That is where he meets with God, and external artefacts are seen not as helping him to focus on the presence of God but as distracting him from such a focus. God, after all, is 'Spirit and Truth'. This same attitude leads to a downgrading of 'external' physical actions such as kneeling or the use of incense or the wearing of vestments in worship. The vast majority of chapels built by Protestants since the Reformation in the UK are plain functional buildings. The author once attended a funeral in a Baptist chapel in Belfast and was astonished that the interior was simply a bare hall. The term 'chapel' is itself significant. Protestants have often been uncomfortable with the use of the term 'church' for a building, for it seems to them to encourage a misunderstanding: for they argue that 'the church' is the body of believers, not a building, and believers can meet God anywhere, in a shack or a field or a beach, they don't need fine buildings. In Wales believers have long been styled as 'chapel' or 'church' people depending on whether they attended worship with the Nonconformists or with the Church in Wales. ('Nonconformists' is a term used to describe those who do not 'conform' to the established or majority religion.) The Church in Wales is the equivalent in Wales to the Church of England in England, but it was split from the Church of England in 1920, owing to the huge expansion of the Nonconformist sects and denomination in Wales over the previous century.

Inward and outward devotion

The difference here from Catholicism is very stark. Catholics on many issues are *both/and* people. Catholics claim that we need *both* the inward *and* the outward. The inward being of the heart is expressed not merely in feelings like hope or joy or fear but in the appropriate gestures. Body and soul are one. Protestants prefer the *either/or* position, tending to speak as if devotion is *either* inward *or* outward and cannot be both. Or at least, the inward is the only one that really matters. This has much to do with the way that Protestants view the question of how Christ's coming really changed things with regard to Judaism. For Protestant apologists, Christ's teaching differed most fundamentally from Judaism in this: Judaism was a legalistic and mechanical system of practices from which Christ came to save us with his message that God wants loving repentant hearts, not the empty performance of mechanical rituals. This understanding is based on New Testament passages like the one in which Jesus mocks the Pharisees for their reliance on phylacteries (*Mt* 23:5) or washing rituals (*Mt* 7:3). It is also based on statements in the writings of the Old Testament prophets which seem to imply that God does not want the holocausts and sacrifices of the people of Israel but penitence and purity of heart and moral reformation (eg *Is* 1:11). For Protestants, Jesus came to preach a true inward religion of the heart which was to supersede a religion of mechanical performance of external rituals. This religion could be summed up in the two great commandments to love God with all your heart, soul, mind, and strength, and your neighbour as yourself. Naturally for Protestants the sacramental system of the Catholic Church looks very much like the triumph of Judaism within the Church. In their view, far from going beyond Judaism, the Catholic Church has actually succumbed to the spirit of Judaism, creating a second 'mechanical' religion out of the teaching of Christ. This has of course made Catholicism particularly scandalous to those Protestants who think in such a way.

Though the Catholic Church happily accepts that this preaching of an 'inward' religion of the heart was indeed part of the message of Jesus, she does not claim that this in itself constitutes the new message that Jesus brought to the world. She locates the newness of the gospel in the Incarnation, in the idea that God became man. Whereas the teaching of spiritual inwardness was indeed already present in authentic Old Testament Judaism, which at its best was never a merely mechanical religion of ritual performance, it was the astonishing idea that God could take on human flesh that represented the revolutionary unprecedented and scandalous element in the gospel. This accounts for the extraordinary predominance of pictures of the Madonna and Child in western art up to the sixteenth century. It is an image that encapsulates for Catholics the central mystery of Christ's coming – that God the ultimate spiritual being became flesh, and he did it by coming through the womb of a human mother.

Although Protestants do most certainly believe in the Incarnation, there has always been a strong tendency among them to give a greater priority to the importance of the atoning death of Christ as the means for us to obtain forgiveness of our sins. This has been especially marked among those who belong to the movement within Protestantism known as evangelicalism.

The bible read as condemning the Catholic Church

Martin Luther (1483-1546) and John Calvin (1509-1564), the most famous of the leaders of the sixteenth-century Reformation, found their ammunition for their attacks on the Catholic Church in the bible. When they attacked the Catholic Church as having replaced the 'spiritual' gospel of the early church with a 'materialistic' and 'mechanical' sacramental system, they did so on the basis that this 'spiritual' gospel was the only gospel to be found in the bible.

Whereas in the Catholic Church the bible is understood to belong to the Church and is regarded as her book to be interpreted by her collectively through her properly appointed teachers, in the Protestant churches, the bible text became the touchstone by which beliefs and practices were to be evaluated. This has continued to be the case down to the present day. In practice it means that a Catholic who is asked about a matter of faith or morals often begins his answer by saying 'The Church teaches that..'; whereas a Protestant is liable to begin his answer by saying 'The bible teaches that..'. Protestants generally believe that they alone are faithful to bible teaching, arguing that Catholics have added a great many things to the simple bible message. Lists of such things will vary, but generally they include the sacramental system, the centrality of the mass and its sacrificial meaning, pilgrimages and shrines, rosary beads, Marian teachings.

This is confusing for Catholics, who are quite accustomed to regarding the Scriptures as central to the faith of the Church. They see the book of gospel readings carried solemnly in procession to the lectern Sunday by Sunday during mass as an indication of the veneration in which the gospels are held. From the Protestant point of view, however, this kind of symbolic action has nothing to do with actually obeying what is in the Scripture. In a sense it seems a perfect illustration of their accusation that the Church gives outward veneration to the Divine Word while actually ignoring its message - the accusation made by Our Lord himself against the Pharisees. The complaint that Catholics have actually refused to follow the Scripture while claiming it as their own is so fundamental to the Protestant self-perception that it merits further consideration.

What it really amounts to is the claim that each Christian must be permitted to study the Scriptures personally as a set of books. When the medieval Church is attacked for having kept the bible from the people, this is what is meant. When considered in the context of the twenty-first century, the attitude of the medieval Church may indeed seem absurd to us today. And Catholic apologists who point out that since the twentieth century Catholics have in fact been encouraged to study the Scripture for themselves merely add fuel to the fire, convincing the Protestant that the Church has finally come round to belatedly accepting the position of the Reformers.

The truth is however that the change of Catholic stance on laypersons and the Scriptures is simply a response to sociological changes that have resulted from the growth of universal education in the western world since the late nineteenth century. In a world where so many can read and where the scriptures are so freely available in cheap editions as the result of advances in printing, the previous restrictive attitudes with respect to the availability of the bible to individual believers have lost any sense. This is not to say that the huge difference between the Protestant and the Catholic understandings of the task of the Church and the role of the layperson has been erased overnight.

The Bible in the Liturgy

For the Catholic, the Church as the Body of Christ is where we live with him, and the task of the believer is to live and pray with the Church as she relives the life and sufferings and death of Christ year by year in the liturgy. The believer is also to access the graces offered in the Church's sacraments which enable him or her to perform acts of charity and love in accordance with Christ's principles. All the liturgies have prescribed forms and it is not necessary to be able to read to participate fully in the liturgy. The Church liturgies are saturated with the bible and represent the fruits of the Church's meditation on the bible.

Long ago the Church divided the sacred text into portions to be given to the people at weekly masses, reflecting the liturgical season, that is, the particular aspect of Christ's earthly life being remembered at that time - eg the nativity stories at Christmas, the passion stories in Holy Week. The Church has already figured out for us what the Scriptures mean, whereas for the individual Protestant it is as if he must reinvent the wheel all over again, checking to see that what is taught actually corresponds to the sacred text. Protestantism is also preoccupied with the idea of reading each book consecutively from its first sentence to the last, whereas the Church presents portions of bible books in relation to each other at mass daily and weekly; she throws light on their meaning in terms of different aspects of the gospel message. The earlier justification for preventing individual believers from studying the bible privately was to be found in fears of what has precisely turned out to be the case: namely, that gifted and glamorous individuals unauthorised and untrained in the necessary skills of interpretation would lead vulnerable persons away from the Church into schismatic movements.

Private study of the Bible

For Catholics it is not the task of the Church to teach the people the contents of a book but to live the life of Christ as a body, worshipping, praying together, and tending the flame of love in the world. The personal practice of bible study is seen as something valuable that can develop and nourish a person's understanding of the gospel and inspire that person to more fervent devotion as long as it is held within the protective boundaries of Catholic believing. It is not however regarded as being absolutely essential to living the Christian life in all its fullness; otherwise how could the millions of illiterates in the world follow Christ? The Protestant by contrast sees it as his task to teach the faithful to study the bible and to understand the bible message, and there is a huge emphasis in Protestantism on private bible study. There is one particular Protestant missionary society, the Wycliffe Bible Translators, which is dedicated to getting the precious text translated into all the world's known languages.

With reference to the issue of translation it is worth noting that misunderstanding of the Catholic position has arisen from the long tradition of the use of Latin. Some Protestants have assumed that this was a means of keeping the people in the ignorance of the faith, an accusation which overlooks an important fact: in the Middle Ages, anyone who could read would have been able to read Latin since the teaching of reading and the teaching of Latin went together. Latin was the language for written documents in the law and theology and university teaching and the different European languages only began to be used as written languages for 'serious' matters in the sixteenth century and partly as a consequence of the Reformation.

There is then a huge difference between the Protestant and the Catholic about how important private bible study is for the believer, but there is another issue which is not really addressed by Protestants: the question who is to interpret the Bible? For the Catholic, the bible is interpreted, expounded, and taught solely by her appointed teachers. The Catholic faith does not belong to any individual but to the whole Church, and if any individual interpreter teaches a meaning of the bible which is not in accordance with the Church's faith, the Church's appointed authorities are obligated to remove such an individual from the position of being an official Church teacher. This obligation is owed to the mass of the lay faithful who are not instructed in theology and who are therefore vulnerable to being led astray. For the Protestant the bible is a book 'who runs may read', it is a book given by God as a gift to the human race and it contains his revelation of himself. It was the ambition of the English Reformer William Tyndale (c1494-1536) who made the first translation of the bible into English, to put the bible into the hands of every ploughboy. The bible is believed to speak for itself and it is argued that in every generation countless individuals have met with God as they studied its pages. The fact that this intense experience resulting from study of the sacred text in the absence of external controlling authority has led to the founding of a multitude of separate movements and denominations is - as we have seen - not of great concern to Protestants today. For they believe in an inner invisible unity among believers who agree on the essentials and disagree only on secondary issues.

'The core' and the 'non-essentials' of the gospel

This division between fundamentals and secondary issues is of enormous importance in Protestantism. One of the most important reasons that Protestants give for remaining out of communion with the See of Rome is that the authority of the popes is at best one of the 'non-essentials'. They simply do not need Rome. Many of them will claim that they are in communion with her anyway - in the only sense that really matters, that of the 'invisible' unity which underlies the divisions between the different Christian movements. Many others will argue that they have a mission to offer a more authentic Christian alternative to Rome, so could never conceive of assenting to the authority of the Popes. But it is their theory of the core and the non-essentials that enables them to hold to the idea of an invisible unity which transcends any outward disunity among them. Baptism for example has been an ongoing battle ground in the Protestant movement down to the present time. A sizeable proportion of Protestants do not accept the practice of infant baptism. This is in fact the reason behind the label some denominations have of 'Baptist' Churches. Baptist Churches are convinced that the need for the individual to give assent to the call of Christ from the heart is so essential that nobody can be accepted as a fully-fledged believer until they reach adulthood, at which 'believers' baptism' is practised by full immersion. Others like the Presbyterians and the Anglicans point to evidence in Scripture that whole families were baptised - which must have included children, and understand that children are 'covered' by the faith of the parents. This difference in practice is not nowadays generally regarded as a difference of 'fundamentals' - though in earlier generations it might well have been. The question of the core versus the non-essentials has not remained static in the centuries since the Reformation. Over the past hundred years in mainstream Protestantism what is considered to be the non-negotiable core has shrunk. At one time belief in the Holy Trinity would have been considered essential for someone to be called a Christian, but nowadays Unitarians - who split away from the mainstream on precisely that issue - may well be welcomed into ecumenical gatherings and Quakers too - though their doctrinal base and liturgical practice is virtually non-existent.

At the same time there has been a noticeable movement away from doctrinal clarity and towards a more 'touchy-feely' approach to religion in which personal experience has attained a greater importance. To a great extent this reflects changes in the general ambient culture; a Catholic priest had a discussion with a young lady regarding a proposed wedding venue. She requested a suitably exotic location, and the priest consulted his bishop about it. The answer was that it was not in accord with canon law. When informed of this, the lady replied 'It's *right for me*, Father'. In a similar vein, a Protestant cleric informed the present author that he 'was *not prickly*' on moral matters. Intercommunion at ecumenical gatherings has become the norm for all Protestant participants and doctrinal differences that previously would have prevented this are largely ignored today. The refusal of the Catholic Church to come into line with the Protestants on this is widely resented.

For the Catholic the distinction assumed by Protestants between the 'core' and the 'non-essentials' begs the important question 'who is to make the distinction?' The problem is that for the Catholic Church allegiance to the See of Rome is a fundamental core issue whereas for Protestants it is not. But the division goes much deeper, for generally speaking Protestants restrict their notion of what has been revealed much more drastically than the Catholic Church does. Though the general moral principles contained in biblical passages like the Sermon on the Mount are of course taken to be revealed, Protestants do not accept that there is binding revelation in matters like abortion or contraception, which for them are largely left up to the individual. Where contraception is concerned this represents a shift in opinion from earlier times when it was universally condemned. There has also been a shift in opinion regarding divorce, which is becoming increasingly acceptable in Protestant circles where it was outlawed before the War. For the Catholic Church revelation comes to us through the teaching of the Church and it covers many more particular areas of morality.

Authority

A major area of difference between Catholic and Protestant concerns the nature and scope of authority in the Church. For Catholics the Pope together with the hierarchy of bishops forms the ultimate authority and Catholics are expected to accept not just the doctrinal teachings of the Church, but also the moral teachings, which may prove very costly for some to follow - especially in the area of marriage laws. The Catholic Church could be defined as the global network or community of those who are in communion with the See of Rome. The Church is like a wheel, the local churches are on the circumference, each one is linked to Rome in the centre but by virtue of their shared centre they are also linked to each other. Protestants do not see the need for such centralised authority and believe that Catholic obedience to the Pope infringes the liberty of the individual. A common Protestant objection to the Catholic Church holds that an individual who submits to the Church throws away his personal freedom to dissent or to develop original ideas. In the Protestant movements authority is exercised in all kinds of ways. The state churches of northern Europe - Lutheran and Anglican - have retained bishops, but in the case of England the authority of the bishops has been absorbed into that of the General Synod, in which decisions are taken by counting heads. In the Scottish Presbyterian Church the authority of the ministers is greatly circumscribed by that of the lay elders who surround him. In the Methodist Church the minister stays only for a limited period in one place and is obliged to move on at the end of that period. In Anglican parishes the authority of the vicar is balanced by that of the lay members of the parochial church council who are elected from the congregation. In some Brethren churches there is no minister and services are taken by laymen in rotation. One thing all of these hugely disparate movements have in common is a rejection of 'priestly power' as cherished in Catholicism. Whereas according to the Catholic Church the priest has the power (derived from the Apostles) to forgive sins and also to bring about the transformation of the bread and wine of the eucharist into the body and blood of Christ, the Protestant cleric or minister is primarily a spiritual teacher and a pastor, and the line between clerical and lay is nowadays becoming increasingly blurred. In one part of Australia where evangelical Anglicans are very strong, there is an insistent movement towards allowing lay celebration of the eucharist. The ordained minister is seen as special not by virtue of unique graces given to him or her through the Church at ordination, but only by virtue of his special training, particular gifts and charisms, or particular knowledge and experience.

Where the authority of the pope is concerned, the average Protestant is simply bewildered. He cannot see the need for a single all-embracing authority in the Church anyway, and the notion of an infallible authority seems very strange to him. Evangelicals are happy with the notion of an infallible book - the bible, - but not with that of an infallible person. In fact the notion of an infallible person is felt to be much trickier and more worrying than that of an infallible text. The reasoning goes that Scripture is once-given divine revelation and contains all we need for salvation. Why do we need an infallible interpreter when we have the infallible text?

Our Lady

One of the most distressing aspects of Protestantism for Catholics is the absence from its teaching of Our Lady. The classic Protestant arguement on Our Lady runs roughly like this: she was an ordinary young girl - a sinner like everyone else apart from Christ - plucked from obscurity by a divine *fiat* to perform the task of giving birth to God's incarnate Son. The point about her is her very ordinariness, and she herself wanted nothing more than to point us to her Son and his work. 'There is one Mediator between God and man, the man Christ Jesus' (1 *Tm* 2:5). Having done her work she withdrew into obscurity, allowing her Son's glory to shine out. She was in no way exempt from human sinfulness, and indeed this is actually the main point about her - God chose to become incarnate of and among sinful humans. The last thing she would ever have wanted would be the veneration paid her by Catholics. She is seen as a figure of history to be treated with massive respect, the author of a supremely important act, but now superseded by the glory of her Son. Protestants do not address prayers to Our Lady, but this is part and parcel of their approach to the dead in any case, for they do not address prayers to the saints either, nor do they pray for the dead. It is considered that deceased persons are entirely in the hands of God and his mercy; from that point we cannot influence their destiny in any way. This is connected to the Protestant rejection of the doctrine of Purgatory. For Protestants there is only heaven and hell and no intermediate possibility. As for asking the prayers of the saints, Protestants do not make a distinction as Catholics do between 'ordinary believers' and 'saints'. In the New

Testament the term for 'saint' is used simply to designate 'believer' and this is how Protestants customarily understand it. We have here a classic example of how Protestants prefer to reattach words to their bible meanings, eschewing later semantic developments. For them no church has the authority to proclaim that a particular individual is a 'saint' in the sense of a person set apart by that person's heroic charity or exceptional devotion to Christ. They consider that to introduce this kind of 'hierarchy' among believers is not merely undesirable but damaging, since it makes 'ordinary' believers think they are somehow inferior.

The only concession made by Protestants in this area is to allow that certain Christians in the past have excelled in their faith and are worthy of being memorialised in art and sometimes in commemorative services. The Church of England Prayer Book liturgical calendar retained special mention of some medieval saints, of whom the latest was St Richard of Chichester. More recently names of celebrated Christians of modern times have been added as being worthy of commemoration.

The Great Divide in Protestantism: Evangelicals and Liberals

Evangelicals

Broadly speaking the main dividing line within Protestantism is between the evangelicals and the liberals. Within the Church of England for example these two ways of thinking are represented by two weekly newspapers - *The Church of England Newspaper* for the evangelicals, and the *Church Times* for the liberals (though at one time the Church Times was the organ for the High Church party). The evangelicals are the heirs to the British sixteenth-century Puritans, to a movement known as Pietism in eighteenth century Germany, and to eighteenth-century Methodism inspired by John Wesley. The evangelicals have been the most powerful, vibrant and expanding movement in the Protestant denominations since the War. Confusingly, there are congregations and denominations that label themselves specifically as 'Evangelical' (eg the *Federation of Independent Evangelical Churches*), but in reality the evangelical way of thinking can be found to a greater or lesser extent among the membership of virtually every denomination. It is not a particular denomination but a way of thinking about the Christian faith. One of the most prominent evangelical movements in the UK today is the Alpha Movement, which comes out of the evangelical Anglican parish of Holy Trinity, Brompton in London. What evangelical Protestantism considers to be the core of the Christian faith is as follows. The foundation of everything is the Bible, considered to be the inspired and inerrant word of God, the place where God has revealed himself to the world and where he is to be sought today. Although all Protestants theoretically pay high regard to the bible, it is the evangelicals supremely for whom the bible is the authority in life's choices and decisions. Prayerful consultation of the bible is always recommended to those about to make any important decision.

The core of the evangelical worldview is however what has been caricatured as 'the telephone line to God'. This is the belief (which is in fact shared by not a few Catholics) that the believer can carry on an ongoing conversation with God, seeking his guidance in every choice and decision, and receiving that guidance especially through attention being drawn to specific bible verses that seem to bear on the issue, or through the words of other believers, or even through dreams. There is a characteristic vocabulary that accompanies this way of thinking: it includes phrases such as 'The Lord has told me that…' or 'The Lord led me to do so and so'. What is special about this way of thinking is the frequency with which God's intervention is associated with 'miraculous' occurrences. God's intervention is often looked for in areas like miraculous healings or deliverances from crisis situations. Some even report enjoying lives lived as a continuing flow of miracles. Extraordinary coincidences are considered to be proofs of God's existence and his ongoing care for us.

But there is a more worrying side to this way of understanding the faith. The author recalls a debate some years ago with an evangelical named Michel. Michel did not take kindly to the idea of someone disagreeing with him and ended the conversation with the frightening rhetorical question: 'Who are you to disagree with what the Holy Spirit has told me?' This draws attention to the issue of the place of reason in evangelical thinking or perhaps to the lack of it. Whereas for liberal and Catholic alike, reason is a God-given gift which we can use with delight, for the evangelical sudden intuitions, insights, prophecies, references to bible verses, or even dreams may trump whatever reason suggests. There is of course support for this in the bible and in the lives of some of the Catholic saints. In the Catholic Church however there is always the external check of the higher authorities to act as a balance to the excesses of religious mania, whereas in Protestant evangelicalism there is nothing to prevent a fanatic from breaking away and bringing over whoever he can to form a new denomination.

This raises the issue of fragmentation and division, a process to which evangelical churches are particularly vulnerable. If a member of a denomination is seized by the overwhelming importance of a particular text or passage or group of passages which he feels his pastor or denomination is neglecting, he may well move to another Christian community or denomination or even found a new one. The loyalty is to the bible as the inspired Word of God rather than to the community. If an individual receives what he understands to be a call from God to do a work, that call will be regarded as imperative even in the teeth of indifference or opposition from those around him or those in authority. This contrasts with the Catholic understanding, which is that those who are seized with a call from God must be patient to allow the Church to pass her verdict; a call has to be confirmed by the wider community through her representatives. Even St Francis - often portrayed as the archetypal 'free spirit' - sought papal approval for his work.

Personal relationship with Jesus

The themes in the bible which evangelicals particularly stress are these. The life of faith is portrayed as a personal relationship with Jesus. The individual enters into that relationship by expressing penitence for his sins and asking Christ to come into his life as Lord and Saviour. From the point of making that commitment he makes a fresh start, incorporating a period of private prayer and bible study into his daily routine and subjecting all decisions and choices to divine guidance. He attaches himself to a suitable local worshipping community - suitable in the sense that evangelical beliefs are preached and practised there. The focus of worship is on the singing of hymns and sacred songs, the reading and exposition of Scripture, and communal prayer, often mostly extempore. A somewhat disturbing tendency among evangelicals is to assert that 'Christians' and 'evangelicals' are one and the same thing; that all true Christians are evangelicals. Traditionally, evangelical student societies in colleges and schools have styled themselves simply 'Christian Unions' - though this custom has of late become increasingly subject to challenge. There is a publication currently displayed on the bookstalls at the back of many a Catholic church which is a 'Christian holidays' guide. In fact this is devoted almost exclusively to evangelical-run holidays or conference centres or celebrations.

Pentecostalism

The most powerful movement within evangelicalism itself at the start of the new millennium is the Elim Pentecostal or Charismatic movement. This has its origins in the US in the early twentieth Century and it lays a special stress on the gifts of the Spirit. It is believed that every Christian believer is entitled to claim these gifts mentioned in the bible, which include speaking in tongues and interpretation of tongues, prophecy and the interpretation of prophecy, and healing. In recent years there has been the spread of a phenomenon known in biblical language as being 'slain in the Spirit', whereby individuals fall over, especially when touched by an evangelist or pastor, and there are also instances of outbursts of barking or of uncontrollable laughter. Phenomena of this kind have become familiar to a minority of Catholics who are involved in the Catholic Charismatic Movement. Persons in this movement often have joint prayer meetings with Protestant Charismatics, and this has led to an unprecedented rapprochement between some elements in evangelicalism and Catholicism. The newsletter of the Alpha Course regularly publishes stories of lapsed Catholics who had their Catholic faith renewed through experience of the Alpha Course, and this is something new in recent years. Well into the postwar years, many evangelicals would have regarded Catholics as persons in need of conversion to the evangelical faith and would never have prayed together with them or accepted them fully as fellow-Christians.

Spreading the gospel

Given their enthusiastic commitment to the idea of personal conversion, it is hardly surprising that evangelicals have a huge investment in spreading the gospel. They are keen to mount evangelistic crusades or rallies or calls to revival at which powerful speakers issue an invitation to those present to make a commitment to Jesus on the spot. The Alpha Course is a classic example of this, it is a basic account of the Christian faith as seen from the evangelical perspective which is wholly geared to winning converts. It is not clear precisely why the Alpha Course has been so phenomenally successful, for it is not dissimilar to earlier courses which had nothing like the same impact, but three factors may be important. One is the use made of videos (and now dvds). The production of a video series centrally enables even small churches to run the courses without the need for local resources they may not have. Nicky Gumbel, the Vicar of Holy Trinity Brompton in London, who is featured in some of the videos, is an attractive speaker, and he undoubtedly scrattches where many people itch on issues like 'why organised religion seems boring'. Finally the Alpha course has pioneered the combination of a gospel message with a shared meal.

There is no doubt that this makes human contact much easier and attracts lonely people who are looking for friendship. One criticism sometimes levelled at evangelicals is that they are so keen to communicate the basics of the gospel that they never really take their followers to a deeper level or help them to grow more mature in their faith. Another problem is that in presenting the drama of discipleship and the attractions of knowing Jesus, speakers may fail to prepare converts for the hard graft and struggle involved in carrying the cross with him. Another difficulty with evangelicals is that they do tend to encourage personality cults: a gifted preacher will attract audiences from a considerable area but when he leaves the church, many will drift away. A fine Anglican evangelical preacher of the sixties and seventies who died tragically young was David Watson. He took over a sparsely-attended church in York and built up Sunday attendances of nine hundred. However it was said that many of those who came were not converts but 'commuters' who abandoned their own churches in other parts of the city and surrounding areas in order to come and sit at his feet.

A private gospel

There is a much deeper problem with evangelical teaching. Classically it proclaims 'the God of the Bible' over against 'the God of the Church'. Evangelicals say that the gospel is a personal relationship with Christ, the Christ of the Bible, and that church is secondary. The Christ of the bible is said to be an unfailing friend and support and the source of joy and peace even when the church is a disappointment. Sometimes they say they are preaching 'not religion but Jesus'. The believer is encouraged to look for Christ above all in his personal 'quiet time' of bible study and private prayer. What counts above all is his personal decision to 'accept Christ into his life' and 'become a Christian'. Once he has done that, he is to look for a 'bible-believing' church to join; if that church falls into the hands of an 'unconverted' pastor he is at liberty to move to another. There are even a few who say that they have given their lives to Christ but who do not attend any church; claiming that they haven't found 'the right one' or 'the one where the gospel is preached'. In other words, this gospel is basically a private one, it is based on 'my personal relationship' with Jesus and 'my walk' with him, not on my membership of the Body of Christ. In the Catholic understanding it is not the individual who decides he has become a Christian but the Church who extends membership of the Body of Christ to him; this he receives in receiving her sacraments. For Catholics the practice of the faith once received is moreover communal, we find God together, and attendance at the mass is the first priority even over private prayer, important though that is considered to be.

One of the reasons why evangelicals are so vehement about the idea of 'having a personal relationship with Jesus' is their distaste for 'nominal' religion. Evangelicalism is above all a reaction to the 'state church' idea which has predominated in England and Scotland, northern Germany, and Scandinavia since the Reformation. When the rulers of these territories withdrew their obedience from the Pope and split from Rome, the churches stopped being answerable ultimately to Rome and became answerable to the state. The national churches of these territories tended to equate being a disciple of Christ with being a good citizen, and church attendance became to a great extent a matter of convention. Because each church was a national church that did not receive spiritual input from outside, they tended to turn inwards and suffer a loss of vision. There were breakaway evangelical-style groups from the national churches from the beginning, but the process began to accelerate from the eighteenth century. In Great Britain the itinerant preachers John Wesley and George Whitfield were the archetypal evangelical apostles. The fact that they were itinerants who travelled around the country to speak is itself highly significant. The Established Church of England had no structure to allow this, the parish system meant that each parish priest was a king in his domain and visitors could not preach in his church without his permission. A great deal of corruption had crept into the system and many vicars or rectors were absentees, receiving the emoluments that went with their job but subcontracting the actual work to a poor curate who was paid a pittance. Wesley and Whitfield were obliged to speak out of doors, calling men and women to personal conversion and a deeper spiritual life. John Wesley had no desire to leave the Church of England, but the spiritual movement he founded developed after his death into the separate denomination known as Methodism, which subsequently spread all over the world.

The rise of Methodism is just one example of the constant process of fragmentation which involves groups of individuals splitting off from the state churches to found independent Christian sects or denominations. This fragmentation began in the early days of the Reformation and has continued its relentless advance ever since. It is often claimed by Anglicans that the Church of England is the religion of the English people *tout court*, a claim that was repeated in a recent article in *The Catholic Herald* by Anglican cleric Peter Mullen. Though they usually make this claim as part of an anti-Catholic polemic, these Anglican apologists happily overlook the fact that multitudes of Englishmen and Englishwomen have followed one or other of the hosts of Protestant sects for many generations, and have done so out of the conviction that the Established Church is too stultified and ossified and devoid of spiritual life to be called truly Christian. I have in my possession a gazetteer of English towns and villages published in 1835: it shows that already at that date large numbers of communities had several Nonconformist chapels alongside their Anglican parish church. It is not unknown in the writer's experience for these 'Non Conformists' to claim that they have more in common with Catholics than with Anglicans. And this is understandable, for they are at one with Catholics in rejecting the concept that the spiritual power may be subjected to the temporal, the Church to the state. The conviction that believers must be free from state interference was one of the reasons why the seventeenth-century Pilgrim Fathers emigrated from Britain to America; they crossed the Atlantic in search of freedom.

Non-denominationalism

In more recent ecumenical times the existence of so many different Protestant denominations has had a curious new effect. Individuals now often feel that the only way to be true to the authentic spirit of Christ is to start again with a 'Christian fellowship' which does not belong to any denomination but where 'the gospel is preached'. Often these fellowships meet in private houses and are known as 'house churches' or in leisure centres or community centres, when they are known as 'community churches'. Although the motivation behind the creation of these new movements is entirely understandable, it has to be admitted that they are actually new denominations whether they like it or no. We often dislike labels that are attached to us, even in spite of the fact that those labels may be accurate. The individuals concerned in such communities as these are invariably attempting to recreate something on the lines of the Early Church as they see it described in the Acts of the Apostles.

For Catholics there is a fundamental lack here of what we would call 'ecclesiology' - any notion of what the Church is and of how she must have priority over the individual. In evangelicalism it is down to the individual to decide which church is best or most 'helpful' or most 'biblical' but this makes the individual the judge of the faith, whereas the Catholic argues that it is the Church's faith. Evangelical Anglican clergy have been known to justify remaining in the Church of England despite its many weaknesses from their point of view on the grounds that it is 'the best boat to fish from'. For its place of the Church of England at the heart of the English Establishment brings with it many opportunities for contact not only with the elite governing classes who might otherwise be difficult to reach but with many ordinary folk who come for baptism of their children or their wedding or for funeral provision. It is after all 'mainstream religion' in England. But from the ecclesiological point of view such a statement is very revealing, for it shows that the question of the nature of the Church is way down on the list of evangelical priorities.

Liberals

In addition to being a reaction against 'official' religion, evangelicalism is also hostile to 'liberalism' in religion. Although Evangelicals generally have the fervour and the numbers and the money, the liberals are the darlings of the media and the chattering classes and they are very well represented in positions of leadership not only in the Church of England but often also in other denominations. Whereas the evangelical mindset is ardent, vocal, and often audacious, the liberal will tend to be quieter in his enthusiasm, more measured and more cautious. For the liberal the bible is an authority, but it must be used with caution, it is a document that was produced at a certain historical era not exempt from the prejudices of the day. The seeming lack of support in the bible for the idea of giving women positions of authority in the Church or for looking favourably on homosexual relations is taken to be a result of the prevailing culture that produced the bible. As times change, so does culture and mores, and we must read the bible more for general principles - like those of inclusiveness, tolerance, openness, and generosity of spirit - than for particular moral prescriptions. Liberals tend to be more cerebral in their religion and the idea of direct communications from God through bible texts or of the Christian life as a quest for miracles is not something they readily accommodate to.

Ecumenism

Liberals share some common ground with the evangelicals on one very important area - that of ecumenism. Individuals in both movements are liable to see the multifarious denominations, sects, and movements within Protestantism as a positive thing; a reflection of the rainbow nature of human communities and societies. However, there is a point at which many evangelicals part company from liberals, and it is on the vexed question of authority. The evangelicals take the bible as their supreme authority, and although they do accept that there are things in the bible which are culturally conditioned and therefore not universally applicable to every generation, this cannot for them contradict the conviction that the Holy Scriptures are the revealed Word of God under whose obedience believers must stand. For liberals, reason and the mores of the day must also be given careful consideration. Evangelicals are not keen to talk about the role of reason, in part because they represent a movement which is all about a personal relationship with Jesus, and in personal relationships reason is not apparently a ruling element.

They are also inclined to see God primarily in happenings, events, and phenomena that are above rational understanding - miracles, inexplicable coincidences, prophecies, dreams, and so forth. But liberal religion is a much more sober affair in which faith is regarded more in the light of being 'sanctified common sense'. Energies are directed not so much towards missions, bible studies, and prayer meetings - the staple fare of communal evangelical life - as towards 'the social gospel', ie charitable activities in the wider community. There is moreover usually much more enthusiasm for ecumenical activities among liberals. Some evangelicals are unapologetically suspicious of ecumenism, seeing it as being about compromise and weakness and the lowest common denominator. They also fear that it sucks away important resources and energies from the prime work of spreading the gospel among the unchurched. A minority may still be found for whom ecumenism involving Catholics is particularly unacceptable, and there are cases where a local evangelical community refuses to join in ecumenical activities because of the involvement of Catholics in them.

Charitable activities

Evangelicals are also much involved in charitable activities, but as they see it their motivation is different. They see a danger in Liberal 'moralism', the idea of doing good because we have to; the idea that 'being a Christian' is equivalent to 'being a good person'. They argue that the real motivation for doing good must be my gratitude to Jesus for all that he has done for me. My heart is filled with this gratitude when I realise that salvation is a free gift which I can do nothing to earn, a gift which came out of the sacrifice of Jesus on the cross, a gift won for me at great cost. Even then I cannot do any good deeds at all unless God gives me the grace. Conversion first, then the gift of grace, then I am empowered by God to become a loving person. Without grace I cannot do it.

For evangelicals there is a contrast between a life of 'trying to be good' (moralism) without access to the empowering grace of God, and a grace-filled life lived close to God who gives us the strength to do the good.

Liberals tend to think less in terms of my being forgiven for my sins and more in terms of my being healed of my inner conflicts and tensions which prevent me from being a whole person. They are more likely to look for psychological explanations of how religion has beneficial effects on the human psyche and indeed to see religion as a human phenomenon, a symptom of man's search for God rather than of God's search for man. They are more sceptical of the truth claims of believers and more ready to accept that Christianity itself is just one colour in the rainbow spectrum of world religions, themselves all symptoms of humanity's search for truth and for God. (Such distinctions as this between evangelical and liberal can of course be found within the Catholic Church, for to some extent they simply represent two different mindsets or temperaments.) Liberal thinking in the Church of England moreover accommodates to liturgical practices at both ends of the spectrum - the High Church Anglo-Catholic and the Low Church. Low Church is not the same as evangelical, a mistake often made by observers. Many Low Churchmen are liberals who relish a 'simple' religion suitable for the 'plain man', having an equal dislike for the 'bells and smells' of High Church Anglicanism and for the emotional conversion talk of the evangelicals.

Liberals are often well-educated and highly articulate, which makes them attractive to the media. It is arguable that they are represented in media programmes like the BBC's 'Thought for the Day' to a much greater extent than is justified by their actual numerical support. They are certainly well represented on the episcopal bench of the Church of England. The media are as deeply hostile to evangelicals as they are to Catholics. No doubt this is not unconnected to the mentality I referred to earlier when I recorded a cleric saying he was 'not prickly' about moral matters. Smooth sophistication and easy tolerance are more welcome in media circles than 'prickly' people who hold to unpopular principles which seem to go against the current of the day.

Contentious Issues

Can a Protestant be 'catholic'?

The term 'Protestant' is not very popular today in the way
that it was in earlier generations. I was surprised when a
Baptist Minister of my acquaintance said 'he did not
think of himself as a Protestant'. This may well be related
to the influence of the ecumenical movement since the
War. The Ecumenical Movement has tended to emphasise
what Christians have in common and to encourage the
notion of accepting the positive in other types of
Christian religion. The term 'Protestant' sounds negative,
it sounds as though a person is primarily 'against'
something. As many Protestant apologists have quite
rightly pointed out, this is not what the term meant
originally, when it had a more positive sense akin to the
idea of 'proclamation' or 'affirmation'. But down the
years the notion of protesting has come to be equivalent
to the idea of being against something, so the change in
the meaning of the term has not been kind to Protestants,
who insist that they do have a positive creed and stance
and do not simply exist to be anti-Catholic, as some
commentators have suggested.

Equally, many Protestants like to emphasise that they see themselves as 'catholic' (with a small c). Robert McAfee Brown's book (cited above) contains a chapter entitled 'The Catholicity of Protestantism'. The way they reason about this is very revealing. They argue that there is a core of Christian belief contained in the creeds of the early church, a core with which they are in full agreement. They find support in a saying of St Vincent of Lerins to the effect that we should embrace whatever has been believed by all Christians everywhere at all times. They make a distinction between 'catholic' and 'Roman Catholic', implying that there is a 'Roman' version of this universal belief: it is this which they reject, not what is truly 'catholic'. They may be in the habit of referring to Catholics as 'Romans'. What this argument shows is that Protestants view the Christian as a person who assents to a set of credal propositions. By contrast the Catholic position is that believing is about belonging - belonging to the Mother Church, the Body of Christ. What counts for Catholics is not what I say I believe, but that I allow myself to be incorporated into membership of that body. And it is in that Body that I find Christ, in the collectivity, the Christian community.

There is a difficulty inherent in the whole Protestant position which is almost never referred to, perhaps out of delicacy. While there is nothing at all objectionable in the notion of the Church needing to be reformed from within, what the Reformers ended up promoting was something entirely different: the idea that there was a better version of the Christian faith that could be practised outside the Roman obedience. They had discovered something better in fact than the historic Catholic Church. It is not difficult to see that from the Catholic perspective this position seems to be inherently self-righteous. Considering that the Catholic Church brought the bible to birth, wrote the early creeds, and spread the gospel across all of Europe, often at great cost to those involved, it seems hard to understand how there could be a better version of the faith outside the Church. To raise this objection is not of course the same as accusing all Protestants of being personally self-righteous. In France for a long time after the Reformation Catholic Apologists, all too aware of this issue, referred to the '*soi-disant Réformés*', 'persons of the *so-called/alleged* Reformed persuasion'. The Protestant reply to this objection would probably be along the lines that in using the term 'reformed', they have in mind primarily the purification of doctrine to bring it back into line with 'simple bible religion' rather than a claim that their moral behaviour is intrinsically better than that of the Catholics. In earlier generations many Protestants would indeed have made such a claim, but in an ecumenical era it has come to seem more than a little impolite or even indecent outside the more extreme currents of evangelicalism.

Anglicanism and Protestantism

There are particular issues for Anglicans around the use of the term 'Protestant'. Addressing a Catholic audience in Rome in November 2006, the Archbishop of Canterbury identified himself with his audience, referring to himself and them as 'Catholic Christians'. The Church of England alleges that there is an unbroken Apostolic succession in its episcopacy, setting great store by the claim that the bishops of the Reformation era were validly ordained by their medieval predecessors. The Church of England also inherited the medieval church buildings and cathedrals which it still uses today. Apparently therefore the Church of England can legitimately claim to be 'the Catholic Church in England'. Many Anglicans reject any notion that they can be described as 'Protestant', claiming that they have as much right to be called 'Catholic' as 'the Roman Church' which queered the pitch by sending in its missionaries to convert people back to 'Rome' after the Reformation. Anglicans have been known to refer to the Catholic Church in England as 'the Italian mission to the Irish'. This argument was however already answered by St Thomas More. Asked why he persisted in rejecting King Henry VIII's breach with Rome when the English bishops had accepted it, his answer was: 'The English bishops may have done so, but not the bishops of France, Italy,

Spain, Portugal, Austria, etc.'. In other words the Catholic Church in any given country is always only ever a part, not the whole. She cannot act independently of the whole Body, and the spokesperson for the body is the pope. Anglicans may be able to demonstrate a continuity in the episcopacy, but of itself this is not enough. The approval and assent of the global church to her position is also necessary. Such approval has never been forthcoming in any official pronouncements or documents whatever may have been the impression conveyed by friendly exchanges between individual Anglicans and members of the Catholic hierarchy. Moreover, the question of what is taught is fundamental. Anglican apologists claim that the same faith was taught after the Reformation, but that is because they have recourse to the core/non-essential distinction we studied earlier. They regard the question of the role of the papacy as 'just an administrative arrangement' but of course the Catholic Church cannot accommodate to that.

In any case, the degree to which the Anglican Reformers modified Catholic doctrine is rarely acknowledged by such apologists for Anglicanism. There are places where the medieval altar stone has been found to have been placed at the entrance to the church building as a threshold, ensuring that the people trod on it when they entered: nothing could be more expressive of the general desire to turn a completely new page and make the cleanest possible break with the old religion.

Moreover the 39 Articles of the Church of England - still its official doctrinal foundation - contain decidedly anti-Catholic statements. John Henry Newman's experience of a vain struggle to reconcile these Articles with traditional Catholic belief was one of the major factors that impelled him towards being received into the Church.

Anglo Catholics

It is true that since the mid-nineteenth century the Church of England has been transformed into an institution that looks a great deal more 'Catholic' under the influence of the 'Oxford Movement'. This is a movement which has sought to turn a page on the earlier 'Calvinist' era and to recover traditional 'catholic' elements of the faith which, it is believed, had been wrongly discarded at the Reformation. The sacramental system was reintroduced, statues and holy pictures and incense were encouraged, along with practices long abandoned such as public processions and pilgrimage to places such as Lindisfarne and Walsingham. At the extreme there were priests who saw themselves as 'papalists', obedient to Rome as far as possible and bound to Rome secretly, but having to wait for the day of corporate reunion when the Church of England would be reunited with the Holy See.

The followers of the Oxford Movement acquired the label of 'Anglo-Catholics' and their church interiors are almost impossible to distinguish from Roman Catholic church interiors. They celebrate 'mass' and wear the appropriate vestments and keep the feasts and fasts and saints' days of the Catholic Church. Though it is certainly true that their influence has led to much greater tolerance of 'catholicising' practices previously outlawed in the Church of England, there is a tendency among Anglican church historians to exaggerate the impact of a movement that has remained numerically limited and strong only in scattered geographical locations in the UK and elsewhere. One Anglo-Catholic cleric contemplating becoming a Catholic reported to the author that he had been shocked, after working for many years in a part of Africa where Anglo-Catholicism was the prevalent form of Anglicanism, to return to England and realise that the Anglican Church in England was 'not like that at all'. (Anglicanism was planted in Africa and Asia - mainly in English colonial territories - by missionary societies of Anglo-Catholic or evangelical persuasion in the nineteenth and twentieth centuries.)

Anglo-Catholicism has in fact been in decline since World War II and this process has been accelerated as a result of recent decisions taken by the Church of England. Several hundred Anglo-Catholic priests and an unknown number of laypersons left the Church of England after the decision to ordain women was taken in 1992; some became Catholics, others joined breakaway Anglican movements, others followed the Orthodox. The result of this is that at the start of the third millennium the Anglo-Catholic movement in the Church of England has been largely shorn of its 'traditionalist' element. Those who remain belong in the liberal camp, though there is a movement within the Church of England known as 'Forward in Faith' which rejects the notion that women can be ordained to the priesthood. This movement has received a degree of recognition from the Church of England authorities in that it has been assigned its own 'flying bishops' whose ministrations are devoted to those parishes which belong to the movement. These bishops operate alongside the established bishops, and several hundred parishes which do not accept that women may be ordained to the priesthood have been allowed to continue to operate as Anglican under the 'flying bishops' who take care of their pastoral needs in place of the 'territorial' bishop.

Conclusion

At the start of the third millennium the Protestant
movements of the world face uneven prospects. In South
America, evangelical and Pentecostal movements are
making huge inroads into traditional Catholic countries
like Brazil. In the US, evangelicalism is very buoyant and
in recent years has acquired a new sense of its power in
the political arena. In the UK, the Church of England has
continued to leak members and the idea of a single
national church alongside a minority of 'Dissenters' is
giving way to the idea of a (quite legitimate) rainbow of
different faiths. A culture imbued with notions of the
priority of spontaneity, informality, and independence sits
as uncomfortably with an Established Church as it does
with the Catholic Church, and the growth of local
independent fellowships seems set to continue. The
numerical and financial strength of evangelicals in the
UK has yet to be reflected in a corresponding political
clout, but that may yet come. There are some signs of it in
the educational arena, where at least one wealthy
evangelical has put large sums into supporting evangelical
colleges. In the ecumenical arena the growth of
evangelical fellowships continues to pose a seemingly

insoluble conundrum. Where Christian groups consider that the private inspirations of the individual must be allowed free rein to the extent even of his breaking away from his fellowship to form a new one, who can ever guarantee the adhesion of any fellowship to an ecumenical plan or programme? Where there is no readiness to accept a central authority, communities cannot take common decisions with any expectations of universal assent by their members to those decisions. It remains difficult to see how any amount of good will can square this particular circle.

The Reformation

The events of the 'Reformation' led to centuries of bitter theological disputes, wars, persecutions and power struggles, and its consequences endure to this day. This booklet looks at the events which led up to the Reformation in Europe, and particularly in Britain. It shows how much that was good was lost in this conflict.

ISBN: 1 86082 385 8

CTS Code: H 505

Informative Catholic Reading

We hope that you have enjoyed reading this booklet.

If you would like to find out more about CTS booklets - we'll send you our free information pack and catalogue.

Please send us your details:

Name ....

Address ....

....

....

Postcode ....

Telephone ....

Email ....

Send to: CTS, 40-46 Harleyford Road,
          Vauxhall, London
          SE11 5AY

Tel: 020 7640 0042
Fax: 020 7640 0046
Email: info@cts-online.org.uk